5 Greatest Moments

5 Greatest Moments

Being Gratefully Present in a Chaotic World

Len Statham

Pathlight Press

Published 2025 by Pathlight Press

ISBN 978-0-9964758-1-5 (hardcover)
ISBN 978-0-9964758-0-8 (paperback)
ISBN 978-0-9964758-2-2 (ebook)

To the Living God,

still whispering parables

through the quiet moments of our lives.

The Map to Moments

Practice Makes Presence: Putting It All Together

Power: Living in the Flow of Presence and Gratitude

Postlude: The Lasting Impressions

Where Meaning Lives: A Companion Guide to Your Greatest Moments

Introduction

This book has been moments in the making. Not just in its writing, but in its living—born from real experiences, small reflections, and the quiet realizations that surface when we stop long enough to listen to our lives.

The Five Greatest Moments isn't a theory or a motivational slogan, it's a practice. A lens. A way of moving through life with presence and gratitude, even when things are messy, uncertain, or bittersweet.

This book was created to offer something simple yet powerful: a way to notice the moments that matter most and to let those moments shape the story you tell yourself about your life.

Woven throughout these pages are *personable parables*— brief, story-driven reflections inspired by my real-life experiences. These parables serve as mirrors, invitations, and reminders.

They aren't meant to give answers, but to open doors, reminding you that your own moments, no matter how ordinary they seem, hold extraordinary meaning.

As a person in recovery and as someone who has spent years working with people in recovery, I've seen how powerful it is when people start paying attention to the meaning in their everyday lives.

This practice emerged from not only my own reflections, but from witnessing what happens when others find strength and hope in moments they once overlooked.

Noticing your five greatest moments each day can illuminate patterns you haven't seen, reveal what truly nourishes you, and anchor you in a sense of meaning that often gets lost in the noise of everyday life.

You might choose to read this book from beginning to end first, simply taking it in, letting the words settle and the concepts unfold.

Or you may decide to pause and reflect as you go, journaling along the way or starting your own daily list of five moments before you even reach the last chapter. Both approaches are welcome; this is your journey, and there's no "right way" to start.

Some will use the book as a quiet companion, revisiting it again in different seasons of life. Others may find themselves diving deep into the practice right away, using the included templates and reflections to reshape how they move through each day.

And when you're ready to begin or deepen your own practice, you'll find some gentle tools at the back of the book to help you catch those fleeting moments and give them a place to land.

Whether you're holding this book during a season of joy, grief, transition, or growth, it will meet you where you are.

My hope is that this book does more than inspire you, it invites you: To pause. To pay attention. To reflect. And to recognize that the life you're living is already full of greatness; it's just waiting to be seen.

Welcome to your Five Greatest Moments.

— Len Statham

The Path to Presence

Every Moment is a Fresh Beginning

T.S. Eliot

Origin: A New Way to Live Gratefully

Life is a series of moments, each one like a brushstroke on the canvas of our journey, adding depth and color to who we are. Some moments shimmer brightly—those big, transformative events that feel larger than life, like a wedding, a milestone birthday, or the day you stumbled upon a deeper sense of faith.

Other moments are quieter but no less powerful—those that shape our character and quietly define who we are.

Then there are the moments of triumph that make us want to dance in the streets—landing that first job, earning a promotion, or achieving a long-held dream.

And let's not forget the shared moments that bind us together in collective memory, like the thrill of the moon landing, the heartbreak of 9/11, the echoes of the Vietnam War, or the electrifying night when Barack Obama became our first African American president.

As unforgettable as these moments are, life is made of so much more. It's the little bits, tick by tock, that weave together to create a life full of richness and wonder.

You might wonder, what does it really mean to live each day using the "5 Greatest Moments" approach?

It means putting on a new pair of lenses – ones that help you catch life in the act of being beautiful, surprising, or quietly meaningful. It's not about fireworks or perfect days. It's about tuning into the everyday magic: the way someone held the door for you, the moment your coffee hit just right, the feeling of remembering and old song at just the right time.

You start to ask yourself not just "what happened today?", but "what mattered today?" and "what did I notice about myself or others?"

Through this process a new kind of gratitude emerges – not one that ignores the hard stuff but one that includes it.

The spark behind this approach came from a handful of moments in my own life, each one a small piece of a bigger puzzle.

Ironically, it came from a moment while watching the television series *Lost*. In the series, the character Charlie knows he will die by drowning, and as he faces his impending death, he takes a pause in the chaos of the moment and pulls out a scrap of paper.

With a pen in hand and time slipping away, he decides to jot down his "Five Greatest Moments." It's a scene full of heart and bittersweet beauty, as Charlie reflects on the little slices of life that truly made him feel alive.

With the water closing in around him, he's not just listing memories, he's savoring them.

From moments of love to those tinged with regret, his list is a quiet, emotional countdown of the things that matter most, especially the love he holds for his beloved Claire, who has always been his heart's anchor.

In that final flicker of time, Charlie realizes that even as his story is about to end, it's not the big events or the grand gestures that matter most, but the simple, meaningful moments that make life worth living. Moments that are, for him, simply unforgettable.

Our moments, like Charlie's, aren't meant to be tucked away for the grand finale. They're meant to be noticed, savored, and celebrated, right here, right now.

While Charlie held on to his memories at the edge of his journey, life's moments are like little fireflies: they shine brightest when we catch them in the present.

*It is often in the darkest of skies
that we see the brightest stars*

Richard Evans

Gratitude in the Light and the Shadows

We often picture our greatest moments as bursts of pure joy, don't we? But here's the thing: if we're always on the lookout for those shiny, feel-good moments, we might overlook the ones quietly waiting in the shadows.

Some of my greatest moments have surprised me amid deep sadness, appearing in the most unlikely times and places.

It's like discovering a spark of light in the darkest night—its glow feels warmer, brighter, and more extraordinary, simply because of the contrast.

And then there are those beautifully simple moments, little whispers from life that call us to another time—a young daughter giggling with her daddy, or an elderly woman in a waiting room who instantly reminds you of your grandmother.

There are also those unforgettable moments etched into memory not by what happened but by how they made you feel, like the heart-racing thrill of your first love and the soul-crushing ache of that first breakup. The sheer joy of triumph when you win at something and the sting of defeat that follows a loss. The wide-eyed wonder of discovering something new...and the bittersweet unraveling that comes with uncovering long-held secrets.

Each feeling, whether sweet or bittersweet, paints the story of who we are.

By keeping these moments close, by capturing them instead of letting them drift away, we deepen our relationship with ourselves.

These fleeting scenes have a way of captivating us, weaving themselves into the fabric of our memories, linking us to other cherished moments that live in our hearts forever.

This is the heart of the Five Greatest Moments practice: to gently train your mind to pay attention, to stay present, and to gather meaning from the life you're already living.

Personal Parable: The Light in Her Eyes

My mother was dying. Alzheimer's had stolen her words, leaving only silence where conversations once lived. The family had spent months by her side, watching as she drifted further away, her memories dissolving like mist in the morning sun.

We received the call from the hospital that said it was time for the family to gather to make important decisions regarding her care.

I walked into her hospital room. She was awake, but something was different. Pain twisted her fragile body, but it was the fear in her eyes that caught me. It was raw, deep—an unspoken terror of what was coming. I sat beside her, took her frail hand in mine, and braced myself for more silence.

Then, in a voice as clear as the sky after a storm, she spoke.

"Leonard, I love you very much."

I froze. The weight of those words, so simple yet so powerful, crashed over me like a wave. It had been so long since she had called me by name, since she had spoken a full sentence, since she had been able to share anything that was truly her.

But in that moment, her love broke through the disease, through the silence, through everything that had been taken from her.

And in that moment, something inside me shifted.

All the hatred, cruelty, and division in the world felt small—so small—compared to this love, this pure and boundless force that transcended pain, memory, and even time.

Gratitude filled me, not for the suffering or the loss, but for the gift hidden within it: this one perfect moment of absolute love.

I held her hand a little tighter, knowing that even in the deepest shadows, light can still find its way through.

That moment would stay with me forever, a reminder that gratitude isn't just for the easy days. Sometimes, it's for the moments that change us in ways we never expected.

Gratitude unlocks the fullness of life when we pause to notice, and in those moments of presence, we realize the beauty of simply being.

Unknown

Gratitude and Presence: Partners in Life's Little Magic

The magic of the 5 Greatest Moments approach lies in the enchanting union of gratitude and presence—a pairing as unique as it is transformative.

Mindfulness is a powerful tool that allows you to anchor yourself in the present moment, embrace clarity amid chaos, and fully experience life as it unfolds. Most mindfulness exercises end there and can be quite powerful.

Many people weave mindfulness into their daily lives, finding a peaceful rhythm in the present moment. Others craft gratitude journals, stitching together the fabric of each day with threads of thankfulness.

But what happens when we combine mindfulness with gratitude?

Synergy of the finest order!

Picture this: mindfulness is like a magnifying glass that brings the tiniest details into focus—each breath, each flutter of a leaf. Now sprinkle in some gratitude, and suddenly, those little moments become gems, shining brighter as you spot them.

With each step, the world becomes a whimsical adventure, where every little discovery feels like a delightful surprise waiting to be celebrated!

Your thoughts are like playful squirrels, zipping around with their endless ideas. Mindfulness watches them from a distance, letting them scamper freely. But gratitude?

Gratitude is the nut in the corner that makes those squirrels pause and nibble with delight.

Together, they guide your mind to notice the treasure troves of positivity that were always there, waiting to be discovered!

And here's where it becomes truly practical:
When you train your mind to look for presence and
gratitude, you're not just collecting warm, fuzzy
feelings, you're also building emotional resilience.

You recognize what's going well, even during your
hardest days, which can help you stay calm in traffic,
be more patient with your kids, or see your co-workers
criticism as feedback instead of a personal attack.

Presence and gratitude make life more beautiful. But
they also make it more manageable, more intentional,
and – dare I say – more joyfully human.

The Pillars of Presence: The Five Greatest Moments Framework

You cannot strengthen the foundation of tomorrow by weakening the structure of today.

Spurgeon

Blueprints for Being: Building Your 5 Greatest Moments

Imagine you're an architect, not of towering skyscrapers or sprawling mansions but of your own moments—tiny yet profound building blocks that shape your day and ultimately, your life.

In this chapter, we're trading blueprints for mindfulness and hammers for gratitude as we construct a framework for being gratefully present.

The tools? A curious eye, an open heart, and a dash of playful intention.

Together, we'll sketch out a plan to identify, embrace, and celebrate your five greatest moments each day, turning ordinary experiences into extraordinary moments.

Let's get building!

The Art of Discernment:
Choosing Your Moments

Let's start with a paradox: life offers an abundance of moments, yet recognizing and celebrating every single one is neither practical nor necessary.

The key lies in discernment—the ability to sift through the flow of experiences and identify the ones that matter most.

This is where intentionality becomes essential. Not every moment needs to be extraordinary to be meaningful. Some moments reveal their significance instantly—a heartfelt conversation, a surprising act of kindness, or an unexpected victory. Others might whisper their importance, waiting to be noticed amid the noise.

The goal isn't to catch every moment but to cultivate an awareness that helps you spot the *greatest* ones. These are the moments that move you, teach you, or simply remind you to pause and appreciate the beauty of life.

But how do you decide? It starts with knowing what to look for. Ask yourself:

- Did this moment make me feel connected to myself, to others, or to something greater?

- Did it teach me something new, challenge me, or inspire growth?

- Did it bring a sense of joy, pain, comfort, or even necessary reflection?

Once you've asked yourself these questions, take a moment to pause and let the answers settle. Reflect on the moments that stand out, no matter how small or fleeting they may seem. These moments don't need to be grand or life-changing—they just need to matter to you.

To make this practice even more effective:

Write Them Down: At the end of each day, jot down the five moments that felt most meaningful. This simple act of documenting them reinforces their significance.

Savor Them: Spend a few minutes revisiting these moments. Allow yourself to relive the emotions, the connections, and the lessons they offered.

Recognize Patterns: Over time, you may notice recurring themes *in* moments that consistently bring you joy, growth, or comfort. These patterns can reveal what truly matters most to you.

Recognizing patterns might be the most important element of this daily exercise as it can help you excise negative or positive bias that we all suffer from when not fully attuned to our lives.

Let's take a closer look at how recognizing patterns can uncover the biases that shape your perspective, helping you see your greatest moments with greater clarity and authenticity.

Negative bias magnifies the storms, while positive bias may ignore the clouds; wisdom lies in seeing the whole sky.

Unknown

Seeing Clearly: Unmasking Bias to Find Your Greatest Moments

Our minds love to play tricks on us, adding their own spin to how we experience life's moments. Enter the sneaky culprits: negative bias and positive bias. These two tendencies shape how we see our days, sometimes tilting the scales unfairly.

- *Negative Bias*: Think of it as the drama queen of your brain, blowing setbacks out of proportion. You could get ten compliments and one bit of criticism, but guess what sticks with you? The criticism. This bias, born from our ancient survival instincts, can make even a great day feel sour if you let it.

- *Positive Bias*: Then there's the eternal optimist, brushing aside challenges with a cheerful wave. While it's nice to focus on the good, this bias might blind you to important lessons or areas that need attention. Too much sunshine can sometimes miss the rain.

Both biases are natural, but they can cloud our view of the moments that really matter. That's why recognizing patterns is so powerful.

When you take a little time each day to reflect, you'll start to notice recurring themes and realize where your mind might be leaning too far one way or the other.

It's like rewriting a story, changing the narrative—a *restory*.

By identifying and addressing the biases that color your perspective, you begin to craft a more balanced, authentic tale of your day. Instead of letting negativity overshadow the good or blind optimism gloss over the lessons, you shape a narrative that truly reflects the richness of your experiences.

This "restorying" process transforms your daily reflections into a meaningful practice of presence and gratitude.

When you unmask the biases that influence your perspective, you give yourself the gift of clarity—a lens through which life's moments appear in their true, balanced form.

By recognizing patterns and "restorying" your days, you cultivate the ability to see the full spectrum of your experiences.

The moments of joy, the lessons from challenges, and the quiet instances of reflection all take their rightful place in the tapestry of your life.

In this practice, you're not just observing your greatest moments, you're honoring them, learning from them, and letting them guide you toward a more intentional, gratitude-filled existence.

Personal Parable—Walking on Air

I had never been good at asking women out. The fear of rejection always loomed too large, and more often than not, I let opportunities slip away rather than risk hearing the word "no."

But this time was different. I had finally mustered the courage—well, almost. Instead of asking in person, I had called her.

Her answer was clear and immediate. "No."

The rejection hit harder than I expected. I spent the rest of the weekend in a fog of disappointment, dreading Monday, knowing I would have to face her at work. I could already picture the awkwardness, the subtle avoidance, the way she might look at me differently now.

My mind ran wild, filling in the gaps with every worst-case scenario it could find.

That dreary Monday morning, I dragged myself in, bracing for the discomfort I was sure awaited me. But to my surprise, she greeted me as if nothing had happened. And then, even more unexpectedly, she said, "Can we talk at the end of the day?"

I wasn't sure what to expect, but I prepared for another round of rejection. Instead, when we finally spoke, she smiled and said something that changed everything:

"I wanted to say yes. I just couldn't last night. But I really like you."

In an instant, everything shifted. The weight of the weekend melted away, replaced by something indescribable. It was as if my feet no longer touched the ground; I was walking on air.

The same world I had awakened to that morning looked completely different now—brighter, alive with possibility.

I realized then how quickly my mind had jumped to the worst conclusion. I had let a single moment, a single word, convince me that all hope was lost. That's the power of negative bias—our brains are wired to protect us by expecting the worst, but sometimes, they get it wrong.

That day, I learned that the stories we tell ourselves aren't always true. And that sometimes, the best moments in life come right after we think we've lost all hope.

We do not see things as they are;
we see them as we are.

Anaïs Nin

The Stories We Tell Ourselves: How Beliefs Color Our Moments

Every moment we live is filtered through the stories we tell ourselves. These stories, shaped by our beliefs, act like invisible lenses, coloring the way we see the world.

The same experience—a rainy day, a tough conversation, or a fleeting smile—can feel entirely different depending on the narrative we attach to it or what we believe about that experience.

Are we the hero overcoming challenges or the victim of circumstances beyond our control? Is a moment a setback, or is it an opportunity in disguise?

Our beliefs aren't just spectators in this process; they are active participants, crafting the meaning of every moment we experience.

The truth is, the stories we tell ourselves aren't always true. They're influenced by our past, our hopes, our fears, and yes, our biases.

But what if we could rewrite those stories? What if we could see our moments for what they truly are: not as our beliefs tell us they should be, but as they are in their raw, unfiltered beauty?

To rewrite our stories, we first need to pause and recognize the ones we're already spinning—those tales shaped by past heartaches, cultural quirks, and the little gremlins of self-doubt whispering in our ears.

These stories can be so sneaky, coloring every moment with their own shade of bias.

But what if, instead of just accepting them, we asked ourselves, "What story am I telling about this moment?

Is it lifting me up or dragging me down?"

This small act of awareness is like wiping clear a foggy window and finally seeing life's moments in their raw, unfiltered beauty.

And then, the magic begins. This is where we step into the *restorying* process—not by erasing the past, but by playfully rewriting it with a fresh perspective.

Think of it as giving your narrative a makeover, swapping the old lens of worry or regret for one polished with gratitude and curiosity.

When we lean into the present moment, noticing the glimmer in the mundane or the lesson in the challenge, we uncover our *Five Greatest Moments* of the day—the tiny treasures that might otherwise slip by unnoticed.

Gratitude becomes our compass, guiding us to the good, while curiosity hands us the magnifying glass to explore even the trickiest of moments.

A frustrating setback? Maybe it's a hidden opportunity. A quiet, uneventful morning? Perhaps it's the space your soul needed to breathe.

By asking, "What beauty can I find here?" or "What lesson might this moment be gifting me?" we shift the story and begin to see our days for what they truly are: a collection of small, shimmering moments that make up the fabric of our lives.

Restorying isn't about crafting the perfect fairy tale, it's about creating an authentic adventure, full of twists, turns, and a few surprising moments of clarity. It's about finding the joy, the growth, and even the humor in every chapter, big or small.

By rewriting our stories and celebrating our *Five Greatest Moments* daily, we're not just living life, we're curating it, turning it into a masterpiece one whimsical, wonderful moment at a time.

Personal Parable: The Stories We Carry

For as long as I could remember, my family lived by unspoken rules—stories written long before I was born. We never questioned them, just carried them forward, letting them shape the way we saw ourselves, each other, and the moments we experienced.

One day in family therapy, the therapist did something unexpected. He turned to my father and said, "I'd like you to move in with your mother for a week."

The room fell silent. None of us saw that coming. My father hesitated but agreed.

When we returned the following week, something had changed. My father looked different—not just in his posture, but in his eyes, in the way he carried himself. We soon learned that during their week together, he and my grandmother had uncovered something profound: the inaccurate beliefs that had shaped their lives.

My grandmother was a product of her time, when parents were told to let babies cry in their cribs, to withhold too much affection lest it spoil the child. She had followed the rules she was given. But my father, left alone in his crib, had written a different story. He believed he was unloved and unwanted—empty-handed when it came to love.

And he carried that belief into his own family, into us.

That week, my grandmother shared her truth. She told him how deeply she had loved him, how precious he had always been, and how much she ached to pick him up. And in that therapy session, she told him again, "I love you. You were never unloved."

My father wept. We all did. I could see love passing between them, dissolving decades of pain in a single moment.

I realized then how powerful the stories we tell ourselves can be. They shape our moments, define our relationships, and sometimes imprison us in narratives that were never true to begin with. But when we uncover them—we question, rewrite, and reclaim our truth—we free ourselves.

That moment taught me something I will never forget: love was always there. We just needed to see it.

Practice Makes Presence: Putting It All Together

*The Difference Between Ordinary
and Extraordinary Is Practice.*

Vladimir Horowitz

Your Daily Guide to Finding Life's Greatest Moments

Life is made up of moments—fleeting, often unnoticed, yet profoundly impactful when we choose to see them.

Each day offers us countless opportunities to pause, connect, and reflect, but in the rush of daily life, it's easy to let them slip by.

The *Five Moments Framework* invites you to slow down and intentionally tune in, transforming ordinary days into meaningful chapters of your story.

This framework isn't about perfection or seeking grand, life-altering experiences. It's about noticing the small moments that bring joy, spark growth, or offer a challenge worth reflecting on.

It's about being present enough to recognize these moments, grateful enough to embrace them, and intentional enough to learn from them.

By following these simple yet powerful steps, you'll learn to uncover the beauty, lessons, and connections woven into your everyday experiences. With practice, the *Five Moments Framework* becomes more than a daily routine—it becomes a way of living with clarity, gratitude, and authenticity.

Let's take a look at the five steps that will begin your journey.

5 Greatest Moments—5 Steps

1. *Pause:* Stop and create awareness of your day.

2. *Choose:* Discern which five moments matter most.

3. *Write:* Anchor them in your memory by documenting them.

4. *Savor:* Reflect on their meaning and impact.

5. *Recognize Patterns:* Notice recurring themes that guide you forward.

Step 1. Pause and Reflect:
Starting the Foundation

Each day begins with a question:
What stories am I telling myself about my experiences?
Start by taking a moment to pause and become aware
of the beliefs and narratives shaping your day. Is the
setback you faced this morning a roadblock, or is it
a steppingstone? Awareness is the foundation of the
framework, where you wipe the foggy window of your
mind and look at your life with clarity.

How to Practice

Set aside 5 minutes to reflect on moments throughout
your day that stood out. Use prompts like:

What story did I attach to this moment?
Was the story lifting me up or holding me back?

You may also want to add your own questions!

Step 2. Sift Through the Noise: Choosing Your Greatest Moments

Life is filled with countless moments, but not all deserve the spotlight. The key lies in discernment, recognizing the moments that made you feel connected, taught you something new, or brought comfort, growth or even pain.

These are your *Five Greatest Moments*—the ones that matter most.

How to Practice

At the end of the day, identify five moments that stand out to you. They don't need to be grand; they just need to matter. Ask yourself:

Did this moment make me feel connected—to myself, others, or something greater?

Did it teach me something new or challenge me to grow?

Did it bring me joy, comfort, or reflection?

Step 3. Write Them Down: Building Your Story Brick by Brick

The act of writing is transformative. By documenting your five moments each day, you solidify their importance and weave them into the narrative of your life.

This simple practice turns fleeting experiences into lasting lessons.

How to Practice

Keep a journal dedicated to your *Five Greatest Moments*. Write a brief description of each one and reflect on why it was meaningful.

Step 4. Savor and Restory: Shaping the Narrative

Revisiting your moments allows you to uncover patterns and address biases. Negative bias might magnify a mistake, while positive bias might ignore a crucial lesson.

By examining your moments with curiosity and gratitude, you can rewrite the narrative to reflect a more balanced truth.

How to Practice

Revisit your five moments at the end of the week and reflect on the following questions:

Am I focusing too much on the negative and missing the good?

Am I overlooking lessons in favor of easy wins?

Reframe moments to see their hidden beauty or growth potential.

Step 5. Recognize Patterns:
Seeing the Bigger Picture

Over time, your reflections will reveal recurring themes in your life—what brings you joy, what challenges you, and where you find connection.

Recognizing these patterns gives you the clarity to align your actions with what truly matters.

How to Practice

Look back at your journal monthly to notice trends and ask yourself questions like:

What types of moments consistently make my top five?

Are there recurring biases shaping how I view my day?

Use this insight to shape your days with intention, aligning your actions with the moments that inspire, challenge, and bring true meaning to your life.

For many of us, our daily lives become a cycle of responsibilities – working, parenting, caregiving, managing routines. It's easy to lose sight of what fills us up. This practice helps you reconnect to the deeper 'why" behind your days.

Whether you're stuck, burned out, or simply unsure of where your energy goes, your Five Greatest Moments become a compass. They remind you not only of what you're doing, but why it matters – and what makes you feel truly alive.

The *Five Moments Framework* isn't just a practice—it's a way to restory your life. By pausing, reflecting, and rewriting your narratives, you're not just living each day; you're curating it.

The setbacks become opportunities, the mundane becomes meaningful, and your *Five Greatest Moments* become the cornerstone of a life rooted in gratitude and presence.

Each day is an adventure, filled with moments waiting to be noticed and celebrated.

By following this framework, you're building a life, not of perfection, but of authenticity—a life where each chapter is guided by connection, growth, and joy.

Your moments become your masterpiece, and your story becomes uniquely, beautifully yours.

Power: Living in the Flow of Presence and Gratitude

*Always hold fast to the present.
Every situation—indeed, every
moment—is of infinite value,
for it is the representative
of a whole eternity.*

Johann Wolfgang von Goethe

Five Moments a Day: The Key to Mental, Emotional, Physical, and Spiritual Balance

Life moves fast—too fast, sometimes. One minute you're sipping your morning coffee, and the next, you're wondering how the entire day slipped through your fingers.

But what if, instead of letting life rush past, you could capture small but mighty moments—five a day, to be exact—that anchor you in presence and gratitude?

This practice isn't just about collecting highlights for a mental scrapbook. It's about something deeper: a way to recalibrate, to find balance in a world that often feels like it's spinning a little too fast.

And balance, as it turns out, isn't just about standing on one foot without falling over—it's about tending to all the parts of yourself.

Your mind craves clarity, your emotions long for steadiness, your body needs care, and your spirit seeks meaning.

Think of these as the four currents that carry you through life, each one shaping how you experience the world. When we start paying attention to our greatest moments, we begin to see how these currents flow together, sometimes gently, sometimes with force, but always moving us forward.

In the next chapters, we'll take a playful (but practical) journey through each one—because balance doesn't have to be a serious business. It can be as simple as noticing a kind word, a deep breath, or the way the sun hits the kitchen counter just right.

So, let's begin. First stop: the mind, where clarity, presence, and the art of not overthinking everything awaits.

Training Your Brain for Gratitude: The Neuroscience Behind the Five Greatest Moments

Gratitude isn't just a feel-good idea, it's a neuroscientific superpower. The way you train your brain to recognize and appreciate your *Five Greatest Moments* each day has a profound impact on your clarity, presence, and even the art of not overthinking everything.

Researchers in positive Psychology, like those from the Greater Good Science Center at UC Berkely, have found that consistent gratitude practice can lead to increase mental clarity, improved sleep, and even reduced stress.

But this practice isn't just about seeing the good, it's about strengthening your ability to navigate challenges, reframe struggles, and build resilience in the face of life's uncertainties.

By actively noticing these moments, you're not just recalling good things, you're rewiring your brain to find steadiness in the chaos, recognize meaning in difficulty, and focus on what truly matters, even when life is hard.

This doesn't mean ignoring pain or hardship; rather, it gives you a way to move through challenges with greater perspective and strength.

This all comes down to neuroplasticity: your brain's ability to reshape itself based on repeated thoughts and behaviors. Every time you pause to recognize a meaningful moment, whether it's a deep breath of fresh air, a kind smile, or even finding a small sense of peace in a difficult day, your brain strengthens neural pathways that support resilience, emotional balance, and mindfulness.

Over time, this practice helps you shift from reaction to reflection, from stress to presence, from feeling stuck to seeing possibilities.

Even better? Gratitude activates the brain's reward system, releasing dopamine and serotonin—neurochemicals linked not only to happiness but also to emotional endurance and psychological flexibility.

This means that the simple act of reflecting on five moments each day isn't just a way to cultivate joy—it's a biological hack for developing the inner strength to weather life's storms with greater clarity, presence, and ease.

So, when you take time to notice your Five Greatest Moments, you're doing more than collecting good memories. You're building the mental and emotional muscles needed to move through both the highs and the lows with grace.

Gratitude doesn't erase challenges, but it does reshape the way you experience them, helping you find light even in the darkest moments.

And the best part? The more you do it, the more natural it becomes—turning your 5 greatest moments into not just a habit, but a lifeline, a practice that carries you through both the beauty and the struggle of being human.

Emotional Resilience: Finding Strength in the Five Greatest Moments

Life isn't always smooth. Some days feel like a joyful Breeze; others like an unexpected storm.

Emotional resilience isn't about avoiding the storm, it's about learning to stand in the rain, knowing the sun will return.

And the practice of noticing your Five Greatest Moments each day isn't just about celebrating the good, it's about finding anchors of strength, clarity, and steadiness, even in the difficult times.

But here's something important: not every "great" moment feels great at first. Some of the most profound moments of our lives aren't filled with joy, but with meaning—a difficult but necessary conversation, the courage to face fear, the quiet realization that something needs to change.

Sometimes, greatness shows up in resilience itself—the moment you keep going when you want to give up, the deep breath you take before starting again.

When we expand our definition of what makes a moment "great," we begin to see strength in places we never noticed before.

Resilience isn't built in grand, heroic gestures. It's cultivated in the small, everyday moments—the quiet reassurances, the deep breaths, the choice to show up again even when it's hard.

The power of this practice is that it teaches you to see, name, and hold on to these moments, reinforcing the idea that even in struggle, there is something to steady you, something to remind you that you are still moving forward.

So how do we develop emotional resilience through this practice? How do we train ourselves to not only notice joy but also find strength in all kinds of moments—the tough ones, the bittersweet ones, even the ones that don't feel "great" at first glance?

Think about a day that felt particularly heavy, perhaps one where nothing seemed to go right. Maybe you received difficult news, made a mistake at work, or had a conversation that left you feeling exposed or uncertain.

In the moment, you might have thought, *There's nothing good about today.* But later, when you paused to reflect and identify your Five Greatest Moments, something surprising happened.

You remembered the deep breath you took before speaking up for yourself, even though your voice shook.

You recalled the friend who texted to check in, a reminder that you are not alone.

You acknowledged the moment of realization that a change needed to happen, even if you weren't sure how to make it yet.

You noticed the way you kept going, even when it would have been easier to quit.

You found a moment of stillness—perhaps just looking out the window or sitting in quiet reflection—that gave you space to process.

At first glance, this might have seemed like a "bad day." But through the Five Greatest Moments method, you discovered that it was also a day of courage, connection, and perseverance.

Over time, practicing this method trains your brain to recognize resilience as it happens—not just in hindsight, but in real time.

This is the beauty of the practice. It doesn't erase hard days, but it teaches you how to carry them differently. It reminds you that even in struggle, there are moments of strength and when you collect those moments, they become the foundation of your resilience.

The Role of Rest and Recovery: Using the Five Greatest Moments to Recenter

We tend to think of rest and recovery as something we earn after we've exhausted ourselves, as if stillness is a luxury rather than a necessity. But the truth is, our bodies don't just need movement, they need restoration.

Physical health isn't just about how far we can push ourselves; it's also about how well we allow ourselves to recenter, to pause, to acknowledge the moments that sustain us.

That's where the Five Greatest Moments method becomes a powerful tool—not just for reflection, but for realigning with what our bodies truly need.

When we take time each day to notice and honor five meaningful moments, we create space to recognize the physical signals of exhaustion, renewal, and balance.

Maybe it's the deep breath that loosened the tension in your shoulders. The satisfying stretch before getting out of bed. The nourishing meal you almost ate on autopilot but took a second to appreciate.

The moment of stillness between tasks when your body whispered, *Slow down.* The sleep that felt like a reset instead of just another night gone by.

Our physical well-being is built on these moments. But too often, we rush past them, treating our bodies as something to manage rather than something to listen to.

The Five Greatest Moments method isn't just about gratitude, it's about awareness, restoration, and learning to recognize the signals that guide us toward balance.

How can we use this practice to nurture our physical health? In what ways can five moments a day serve as a guide for rest, recovery, and lasting well-being?

We can use the Five Greatest Moments practice to nurture our physical health by training ourselves to recognize and prioritize micro-moments of recovery—the small, everyday instances where our bodies naturally seek restoration.

Too often, we wait until exhaustion forces us to rest, believing that recovery must come in large, structured ways like vacations or full nights of sleep.

But true well-being is built in the in-between moments—the deep breath that calms tension, the first sip of water after dehydration, the stretch that releases built-up stress.

By intentionally noticing and appreciating these moments, we shift our mindset, allowing rest to become a proactive, integrated part of daily life rather than an afterthought.

This practice also helps us reframe rest as strength, not weakness. Many of us equate productivity with worth and view rest as something we must "earn," but that belief often leads to burnout.

The Five Greatest Moments method disrupts this pattern by showing us that recovery is essential to sustainability.

Just like an athlete performs best when they balance training with recovery, we function best when we honor our body's need for renewal, movement, and stillness in equal measure.

By recording these moments each day, we begin to see patterns in how our bodies seek balance, learning to respond to fatigue, stress, and tension with care rather than resistance.

Through this practice, you begin to recognize that rest is not the absence of doing, but an intentional act of sustaining your energy, focus, and well-being. And as you document these moments, you create a mindset shift, one where prioritizing recovery becomes second nature.

Your body already knows what it needs. The question is are you noticing?

Sacred Moments: Presence as a Path to Meaning and Purpose

Spiritual health isn't just about belief, it's about connection, presence, and a sense of something greater than ourselves.

It's found in the quiet moments of awe, the deep knowing that we are part of something bigger, and the small, sacred pauses where we feel fully alive, aligned, and at peace.

The Five Greatest Moments method helps us recognize and honor these moments, creating space for spiritual depth, awareness, and a sense of purpose in our everyday lives.

Spirituality often feels like something we must seek—something to be found in grand experiences or deep meditations. But what if it's already present in the unnoticed moments of our day?

The Five Greatest Moments practice teaches us that meaning isn't something we have to chase; it's something we learn to recognize. Whether we experience spirituality through faith, nature, human connection, or the simple act of being present, every day holds sacred moments waiting to be seen.

Perhaps it's the warmth of the morning sun filtering through your window, reminding you that life continues.

The unexpected kindness from a stranger that affirms the goodness in people.

The stillness in nature that fills you with peace.

The quiet, internal whisper that nudges you toward your purpose.

The deep breath that grounds you in the now.

These moments—subtle but profound—become signposts of presence, reminders that meaning is woven into the fabric of our lives, not just in extraordinary experiences but in the ordinary ones we choose to honor.

When we take the time to capture five of these moments each day, we cultivate a practice of spiritual awareness, allowing us to move through life with more intentionality, gratitude, and connection.

So how does this shift our spiritual well-being? How does the simple act of noticing Five Greatest Moments a day create a deeper sense of meaning and purpose?

The simple act of noticing Five Greatest Moments each day shifts our spiritual well-being by training us to see meaning in the everyday.

Instead of waiting for profound revelations or life-changing experiences to feel connected to something greater, we begin to recognize that sacred moments are already woven into our lives—we just have to slow down enough to see them.

This practice deepens our spiritual awareness by helping us pause, reflect, and acknowledge the quiet, often-overlooked moments that bring us closer to purpose, connection, and presence.

When we intentionally record these moments, we start to notice patterns: What moves us? What fills us with awe?

When do we feel most connected?

Over time, this reflection helps us understand what truly nourishes our spirit.

This practice also shifts our perspective on life's challenges. When we train ourselves to seek meaning each day, even in difficult times, we realize that moments of strength, grace, and wisdom exist alongside struggle.

This resilience fosters a greater trust in life itself, allowing us to move forward with more intention, peace, and gratitude.

Ultimately, noticing Five Greatest Moments a day transforms the way we engage with life. Instead of rushing through our days, we live them more fully, recognizing that meaning isn't something we have to search for—it's something we allow ourselves to see.

Postlude: The
Lasting Impressions

We do not remember days, we remember moments.

Cesare Pavese

Why Five? The Power of Five in the Five Greatest Moments Framework

Why five? Why not three, or ten? The number five wasn't chosen at random; it carries a natural rhythm, a balance between depth and simplicity, and a connection to how we experience and process the world.

Five sits in the sweet spot between too little and too much. If we chose only three moments each day, we might miss the nuance, the quieter moments that shape our experiences.

If we choose ten, it could become overwhelming, turning a reflective practice into a task. Five is just enough— enough to challenge us to notice, but not so much that it becomes unattainable.

Five is woven into the way we interact with the world. We have five senses—sight, sound, touch, taste, and smell—that shape how we experience every moment.

Many traditions recognize five elements—earth, water, fire, air, and space—symbolizing the completeness of life.

Even our own hands, with five fingers, allow us to create, build, and connect. Five has an intuitive wholeness to it, making it a natural number to ground a daily reflection practice.

The Five Greatest Moments framework follows the same pattern: five moments to recognize each day, and five steps to deepen the practice:

1. Pause: Stop and create awareness of your day.

2. Choose: Discern which five moments matter most.

3. Write: Anchor them in your memory by documenting them.

4. Savor: Reflect on their meaning and impact.

5. Recognize Patterns: Notice recurring themes that guide you forward.

This five-step process mirrors the natural way we process experiences, allowing us to move from awareness to transformation in a simple, repeatable way.

Choosing five moments each day is an act of mindfulness, a ritual that gently reminds us to slow down and take stock of what matters.

Over time, these five moments become the markers of a life well-lived, a series of small but meaningful impressions that shape our journey.

So why five? Because five is just right.

It invites us to notice, without overwhelming. It reflects the natural rhythms of our lives.

And most importantly, it creates a practice that is both structured and sustainable—a daily invitation to live with presence, gratitude, and intention.

The Final Spark: A New Beginning

As we reach the final pages of this journey, we arrive not at an ending but at a threshold—a place where the insights you've gathered become the foundation for what comes next.

The Five Greatest Moments framework isn't just a practice, it's an invitation. An invitation to live with a deeper awareness, to embrace each day as a collection of small, luminous moments that shape who you are and who you are becoming.

The true magic of this practice lies in its simplicity. You don't need to wait for grand, sweeping events to feel the weight of meaning in your life.

You don't need to chase perfection or fill your days with endless pursuits.

Your greatest moments are already happening—they have been all along. Now, you simply get to notice them.

It is my deepest desire that this book has guided you through the art of recognizing these moments, of sifting through the noise of everyday life to uncover the ones that truly matter.

You've learned to pause, to reflect, to capture and savor the experiences that define your days.

You've seen how even the smallest moments—a deep breath, a quiet realization, an unexpected act of kindness, and even a moment of setback—can carry immense significance when seen through the lens of presence and gratitude.

But here's the truth: the power of this framework doesn't come from merely understanding it, it comes from using it. From choosing, again and again, to show up fully in your own life.

So, what happens now?

Now, you take what you've learned and make it yours. You wake up tomorrow with a fresh canvas and a simple but powerful intention: to notice.

To be present for the moments that might otherwise slip by unnoticed. To let gratitude turn even the most ordinary experiences into something extraordinary.

Not every day will be easy.

Some days, you may struggle to find even one moment that feels meaningful. That's okay. This practice isn't about perfection, it's about trusting that even in the quiet, the ordinary, or the difficult, something meaningful is always there, waiting to be seen.

And in time, the act of noticing will become second nature. You will find your moments, even on the hardest days. You will see that beauty, connection, and meaning are never far away.

Your story is still unfolding, and every day offers you five new chances to shape it with intention, gratitude, and presence.

So go forth, eyes open, heart ready. The moments are waiting.

And they are yours to claim.

Where Meaning Lives: A Companion Guide to Your Greatest Moments

Instructions for Living a Life: Pay Attention. Be Astonished. Tell About It.

Mary Oliver

Practicing the Five Greatest Moments

Your life is not just made up of big events and milestones. It is shaped by the moments you choose to notice, reflect on, and remember. Some moments bring joy, others bring clarity, and some challenge you to grow.

But all of them contribute to the bigger picture of your life.

This practice is designed to help you pause, reflect, and record the moments that matter. It is not about forcing gratitude or only focusing on the positive, it is about seeing life with more depth and presence.

By engaging with this framework each day, week, and month, you will begin to notice patterns, reframe limiting beliefs, and align your life with what truly fulfills you.

How to Use This Practice
This practice is divided into three parts:

1. Daily Reflection: Capturing the Moments
Each day, take a few minutes to pause and reflect. What stood out to you? What stories did you tell yourself about your experiences? Write down five moments that shaped your day—big or small, joyful, or challenging.

2. Weekly Reflection: Rewriting the Narrative
At the end of each week, look back at the moments you recorded. Do you notice any patterns? Are there moments you need to reframe? This step helps you shift your perspective and deepen your understanding of your experiences.

3. Monthly Reflection: Recognizing Patterns
At the end of each month, take a broader look at your journal. What types of moments keep appearing? What do they reveal about what brings you meaning, challenge, or connection? Use these insights to intentionally shape the coming month.

Begin Today

There is no right or wrong way to do this. Some days
will be easy, and others may feel more difficult. But
every time you pause to reflect, you are training
yourself to live more fully in the present and appreciate
the moments that truly make up your life.

Use the templates that follow to guide your reflections.
Let them serve as a space for honesty, awareness, and
growth.

The Five Greatest Moments
Daily Practice

Date: _____

Each day is filled with moments—some loud, some quiet—that can shape how we see ourselves, our purpose, and the world around us. This practice helps you reflect on the *Five Greatest Moments Framework*, one step at a time.

1. *Pause: Create Awareness*

Take a few deep breaths. Quiet your mind and bring your day into focus.

- What energy am I carrying right now?

- What stories am I telling myself about today?

- Was I present for my experiences, or rushing through them?

Quick Reflection:

_____

_____

_____

2. Choose: Identify the Five Moments That Mattered

What five moments stood out to you today? They don't have to be big, they just need to be meaningful.

Moment 1: _____

Why it mattered: _____

Moment 2: _____

Why it mattered: _____

Moment 3: _____

Why it mattered: _____

Moment 4: _____

Why it mattered: _____

Moment 5: _____

Why it mattered: _____

3. *Write: Anchor Them in Memory*

Take one of your five moments and expand it into a short paragraph.

- What happened?

- How did it make you feel?

- What insight or emotion stayed with you?

Expanded Reflection:

_____

_____

_____

_____

_____

_____

_____

_____

4. *Savor: Sit with What You've Noticed*

Pause again and consider the moments you chose.

- What do they reveal about what matters to you?

- How might you carry one of these moments into tomorrow?

Notes or feelings to carry forward:

_____

_____

_____

_____

_____

_____

_____

_____

_____

5. *Recognize Patterns: Look for What's Emerging*

Over time, reflect on common threads.

- Are certain themes or values showing up repeatedly?

- Is something calling for more attention in your life or work?

(Use this section weekly or monthly to build deeper insight.)

_____

_____

_____

_____

_____

_____

_____

_____

Weekly Reflection: Rewriting the Narrative

Week of: _____

1. Looking Back

   • What patterns do I notice in my moments this week?

   • Did I focus more on challenges or joys?

2. Reframing My Narrative

   • Am I overlooking hidden lessons in my struggles?

   • How can I rewrite any limiting stories?

3. Key Insight from this Week

Reflection:

_____

_____

_____

_____

Monthly Reflection:
Recognizing Patterns

Month: _____

1. Themes from My Moments

   • What types of experiences consistently made my list?

   • What does this tell me about what brings me meaning?

2. Shaping My Future

   • What can I do to invite more of these meaningful moments into my life?

   • How can I use these insights to be more present?

3. My Intention for Next Month

Reflection:

_____

_____

_____

Overcoming Obstacles: Making the Practice Work for You

Not every day will feel easy, and that's okay. Some days, the moments will come naturally, and other days, it may feel impossible to find even one. Practice is not about perfection—it's about showing up.

If you find yourself struggling, here are some common obstacles and ways to move through them.

1. "I Can't Think of Five Moments Today."

Some days feel uneventful or tough, and finding five moments may seem impossible. But this practice is not about finding extraordinary experiences—it's about noticing what is already there.

How to Move Through It:

- **Start small.** If five moments feel overwhelming, begin with just one. Some days, even a single moment of stillness or connection is enough.

- **Shift your focus.** If no "big" moments come to mind, look for the smallest details—a sip of coffee, the sound of laughter in the distance, the feel of fresh air when you stepped outside.

- **Use different senses.** Instead of searching for an event, think about what you heard, saw, smelled, tasted, or touched today. Sensory moments often bring subtle but meaningful connections.

Example:
"I struggled to find five moments today, but I did notice how warm the tea felt in my hands this morning. That was comforting."

2. *"My Moments Feel Too Repetitive."*

Maybe your greatest moments seem to be the same things every day—your morning coffee, a conversation with a friend, a quiet walk. That's not a bad thing. In fact, it may be revealing what truly brings you peace and joy.

How to Move Through It:

- *Lean into the patterns.* If the same moments keep appearing, it's a sign they matter to you. Instead of dismissing them, ask, *what is it about these moments that makes them special?*

- *Go deeper.* Instead of just listing the moment, reflect on what it meant to you. Did it feel different today? Why does it keep standing out?

- *Challenge yourself to look wider.* Some moments repeat because they are part of your daily rhythm, but what else is happening around them? A new observation or small shift in experience may help you see them differently.

Example:
"My morning coffee made my list again, but today I realized it's not just about the coffee, it's about the quiet moment before my day begins. That's what I truly appreciate."

3. "My Negative Thoughts Keep Taking Over."

When life feels difficult, this practice might seem pointless. It's hard to name great moments when stress, loss, or uncertainty are at the forefront. However, these are the times when noticing even the smallest moments of meaning can be most transformative.

How to Move Through It:

- **Redefine what a "great moment" means.** Not every moment has to be joyful; some of the most powerful moments come from growth, resilience, or even grief.

- **Allow room for honesty.** If today was hard, acknowledge it. A great moment might be, "*I allowed myself to rest today when I needed it.*"

- **Find moments of support.** A kind word, a song that resonated, a deep breath—these can all be meaningful moments even in hard times.

Example:
"*Today was tough, but I noticed a stranger held the door open for me at the store. It reminded me that kindness still exists, even on difficult days.*"

4. *"I Keep Forgetting to Write My Moments Down."*

Forming a new habit takes time, and it's easy to forget or put off reflection at the end of a busy day.

How to Move Through It:

- *Attach it to an existing habit.* Link your reflection to something you already do—brushing your teeth, drinking tea, or getting into bed.

- *Use a reminder.* A note by your bedside, an alarm on your phone, or a dedicated journal by your nightstand can help you stay consistent.

- *Make it quick.* If you don't have time for full reflections, simply jot down five words that capture your moments. A longer reflection can come later.

Example:
"I forgot to write yesterday, but today I'll take a moment to reflect on both days before bed."

5. "I'm Not Sure This is Making a Difference."

If you don't notice immediate changes, you may wonder if this practice is really helping. It's normal to feel this way when you're in the middle of building a habit.

Most habits take a little time to settle in – somewhere between a few weeks and a few months – so be patient with yourself. The small shifts you're making now are laying the groundwork for something meaningful.

How to Move Through It:

- *Trust the process.* Just like a garden takes time to grow, this practice unfolds gradually. You may not notice the impact immediately, but over time, you'll start seeing patterns and shifts in awareness.

- *Look back.* Flip through your past entries and see how far you've come. What moments have repeated? What lessons have emerged?

- *Give yourself permission to adapt.* If you need to tweak the way you do this practice—using voice notes, sketching, or sharing moments with a friend— that's okay. What matters is that you stay engaged in some way.

Example:

"I don't know if this is working, but when I looked back on my first week of moments, I realized how much I've been appreciating small connections with people. That's something I wouldn't have noticed before."

Final Thoughts

Practice is not about perfection, it's about presence and awareness. Some days, this reflection will come easily. Other days, it may feel like a stretch to remember even one moment that mattered. That's okay.

What matters most is that you show up—for yourself, for your life, and for the truth of your experience.

Over time, this practice becomes less about writing things down and more about how you move through your day.

You'll start to notice the quiet victories, the brief connections, the small shifts in perspective. Even on the hardest days, there will be something to hold on to— some glimmer of meaning, however small.

Your moments are already happening. They're waiting to be seen, honored, and remembered.

Keep going. This is your story, and you are the one who gets to tell it.